BE A SCIENTIST
LET'S INVESTIGATE LIGHT

JACQUI BAILEY

CRABTREE
PUBLISHING COMPANY
WWW.CRABTREEBOOKS.COM

CRABTREE
PUBLISHING COMPANY
WWW.CRABTREEBOOKS.COM

Author: Jacqui Bailey

Editorial director: Kathy Middleton

Series editor: Julia Bird

Editor: Ellen Rodger

Illustrator: Ed Myer

Packaged by: Collaborate

Proofreader: Petrice Custance

**Production coordinator
and Prepress technician:** Ken Wright

Print coordinator: Katherine Berti

Library and Achives Canada Cataloguing in Publication

Title: Let's investigate light / Jacqui Bailey.
Other titles: Investigating light
Names: Bailey, Jacqui, author.
Description: Series statement: Be a scientist |
  Previously published under title: Investigating light. |
  Includes index.
Identifiers: Canadiana (print) 20200354183 |
  Canadiana (ebook) 20200354256 |
  ISBN 9781427127730 (hardcover) |
  ISBN 9781427127792 (softcover) |
  ISBN 9781427127853 (HTML)
Subjects: LCSH: Light—Juvenile literature. | LCSH: Light—
  Experiments—Juvenile literature.
Classification: LCC QC360 .B35 2021 | DDC j535—dc23

Library of Congress Cataloging-in-Publication Data

Names: Bailey, Jacqui, author.
Title: Let's investigate light / Jacqui Bailey.
Description: New York, NY : Crabtree Publishing Company, 2021. |
  Series: Be a scientist | Includes index.
Identifiers: LCCN 2020045056 (print) | LCCN 2020045057 (ebook) |
  ISBN 9781427127730 (hardcover) |
  ISBN 9781427127792 (paperback) |
  ISBN 9781427127853 (ebook)
Subjects: LCSH: Light--Juvenile literature.
Classification: LCC QC360 .B345 2021 (print) | LCC QC360 (ebook) |
  DDC 535--dc23
LC record available at https://lccn.loc.gov/2020045056
LC ebook record available at https://lccn.loc.gov/2020045057

Crabtree Publishing Company
www.crabtreebooks.com   1–800–387–7650
Published in 2021 by Crabtree Publishing Company

First published in Great Britain in 2019 by Wayland
Copyright © Hodder & Stoughton, 2019

The text in this book was previously published
in the series 'Investigating Science'

Printed in the U.S.A./122020/CG20201014

Every attempt has been made to clear copyright.
Should there be any inadvertent omission please apply
to the publisher for rectification.

Published in Canada
Crabtree Publishing
616 Welland Ave.
St. Catharines, Ontario
L2M 5V6

Published in the United States
Crabtree Publishing
347 Fifth Avenue
Suite 1402–145
New York, NY 10016

BE A SCIENTIST

LET'S INVESTIGATE LIGHT

CRABTREE
PUBLISHING COMPANY
WWW.CRABTREEBOOKS.COM

CONTENTS

What is light?   6

How do we see?   8

Bright as day   10

Light at night   12

Traveling light   14

Bouncing light   16

Blocking light   18

Making shadows   20

Shadow shapes   22

Sun and shadow   24

Shifting shadows   26

Glossary   28

Learning more   30

Index   32

WHAT IS LIGHT?

Light lets us see things. Without light we would not be able to see anything at all.

THINK about the differences between light and dark.

- In the daytime, it is light outside and things are easy to see.
- It is hard to see at night in the dark. We use electric lights to help us.

How well can you see without light?

YOU WILL NEED
A blindfold
(e.g. a scarf or pillowcase)
A friend
Some small mystery objects
A cookie tin or a box with a lid

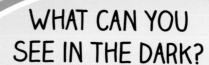

WHAT CAN YOU SEE IN THE DARK?

1 Sit on the floor. Ask your friend to tie the blindfold over your eyes. Make sure you cannot see anything.

" BECAUSE...

You cannot see what your objects are when you are blindfolded because the blindfold has blocked out the light. Light lets us see. Seeing is one of our five **senses**. When there is no light, we use some of our other senses, such as touch or smell, to find out what things are. **"**

4

Slowly lift the blindfold. How far do you have to lift it before you can see if you were right?

3 Double check that there is no light coming through the blindfold. Open the tin or box and take out the objects, one at a time. Try to find out what they are by feeling them. Tell your friend what you think each mystery object is.

2 Ask your friend to put the mystery objects inside the tin or box and close the lid.

HOW DO WE SEE?

We see when light gets inside our eyes.

THINK about how you see.
- When your eyelids are open, light enters your eyes through the dark hole in the middle, called the **pupil**.
- When your eyelids are closed, no light can enter the pupil and you cannot see.

Does the amount of light make a difference to how well you see?

YOU WILL NEED
A mirror
A pencil and paper
A darkened room
A watch or cell phone

HOW DOES LIGHT CHANGE YOUR EYES?

1 Look at your eyes in the mirror.

2 Make a drawing of your eyes to show how big the pupils are compared to the rest of your eye.

3 Sit in a dark room for three minutes. Take a watch or cell phone with you to time yourself.

4 Go back into normal light and immediately look at your pupils again. Compare them with your drawing. Is there a difference? What happens to your pupils as you look in the mirror?

" BECAUSE...

Your pupils are larger after being in the dark because they change size depending on how much light there is around you. When it is dark, they open up as wide as they can to let in as much light as possible. In very bright light, they become as small as they can to stop the bright light damaging the inside of your eyes. "

9

BRIGHT AS DAY

During the day, the **Sun** gives us all
the light we need.

Bright lights
can hurt your eyes.
The Sun's light is the
brightest light of all.
Never look directly at the
Sun because it could
damage your eyes.

THINK about the light
from the Sun.

• On a sunny day, things look
bright and clear.
• When it is cloudy, everything looks
duller but we can still see.
How strong do you think the
Sun's light is?

YOU WILL NEED
A pencil
A sheet of paper

Object	Sunny	Cloudy
water	sparkly	dull

HOW STRONG IS SUNLIGHT?

1 Go outside on a
day when it is
sunny but there
are also clouds in
the sky.

2 Look around you. How does everything
look when the Sun is shining? Make a list like the
one shown above, and note how clearly you can
see things. What do the colors look like?
Do some things sparkle?

" BECAUSE...

When there are clouds in the sky the daylight is dim and colors are less bright. This is because the clouds are blocking out some of the Sun's light. But clouds cannot block out all of the Sun's light because it is too strong. **"**

The Sun's light is the strongest type of light. It spreads for millions and millions of miles through space.

3 Wait for the Sun to go behind a cloud. Now look around you again. What differences can you see? Write them down.

4 Look at the picture above. How do you think this picture would change if the Sun went behind a cloud?

LIGHT AT NIGHT

The sun is a **natural light source**. At night, or in places where sunlight cannot reach, we use **artificial light sources**.

YOU WILL NEED
A pencil and paper
A ruler

THINK about sources of light other than the Sun.
• We use flashlights to help us see in the dark.
• We use electric lights in our homes.
What other sources of light are there?

HOW MANY LIGHT SOURCES CAN YOU FIND?

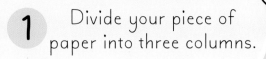

1 Divide your piece of paper into three columns.

2 In the first column, make a list of all the things that give out light, both indoors and outdoors. For example: house lights, candles, and computer screens.

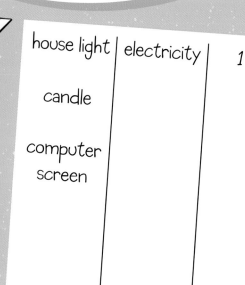

house light	electricity	1
candle		
computer screen		

3 In the second column, write down what makes each light source work. For example: electricity, burning. Ask an adult if you are not sure.

4 In the third column, give each light source a mark out of 3 for its level of brightness: 1 = dazzling, 2 = easy to see by, 3 = hard to see by.

" BECAUSE...

Some things that shine brightly are not light sources. They do not make their own light, but they create **reflected light** when light from another source bounces off them. For example, the **Moon** reflects light from the Sun. To learn more, see pages 16-17. "

" BECAUSE...

Some lights are brighter than others because they are more powerful. The brightest lights are usually electric lights. Light that comes from a burning candle or wood is weak and may not last very long. "

5 Which light sources are the brightest?

TRAVELING LIGHT

Light travels outward from its source in straight lines.

YOU WILL NEED

2 large squares of cardboard

A pencil and ruler

A knitting needle

Sticky tack

A flashlight

A room you can darken

THINK about how you can see lines of light.

- A beam of light from a flashlight is straight. It does not curve or bend.
- In the woods, you can sometimes see lines, or beams, of sunlight shining through the branches of the trees.

Can you see how light travels?

HOW DOES LIGHT TRAVEL?

1 Find the center of both squares of cardboard by drawing across them from corner to corner, as shown.

CENTER

2 Use the knitting needle to make matching holes in the center of both squares. Line up the squares so that you can see through both holes. Prop them up in position with sticky tack.

3 Darken the room and shine the flashlight through both holes. Do you see a beam of light passing between them and through the hole in the last square? Adjust the squares until you do.

4 Now move one of the squares 0.5 inches (1.25 cm) to one side. What happens?

BECAUSE...

When you move one square to the side, the beam of light no longer shines through the last hole. This is because light cannot bend or curve to the side to shine through the hole.

BOUNCING LIGHT

Most of the light we see is reflected, or bounced, off the things around us.

YOU WILL NEED
Objects with different surfaces (e.g. a CD, a straw basket, cloth, a bowl, a block of wood, a mirror, a metal saucepan)
A flashlight

THINK about how different things reflect light.
• A smooth, polished table looks shiny.
• A rough brick wall looks dull.
Which surface reflects the most light?

WHICH SURFACES SHINE THE MOST?

1 Spread your objects on the floor of a darkened room. Shine the flashlight on them one at a time.

2 Which objects shine the most? Do any of them still shine when the flashlight is turned off?

" BECAUSE...

Smooth, flat surfaces shine the most because light from the flashlight bounces off them straight into your eyes. Light bounces off rough surfaces, too. But this light is scattered by the bumps in the surface so they appear dull. None of the objects shine in the dark, because they do not make any light of their own. "

Reflective surfaces change the direction of light. Try this investigation.

CAN YOU MAKE LIGHT TURN A CORNER?

1 Stand just behind an open door.

2 Hold a hand mirror out in front of you and angle it until you can see what is on the other side of the door.

light

mirror

you   door

light from behind the door bounces off the mirror

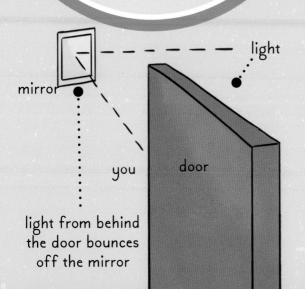

" **BECAUSE...**

You can see what is on the other side of the door because the light from that side hits the mirror and bounces off it at an angle, into your eyes. "

17

BLOCKING LIGHT

Light passes through some things, but not through others.

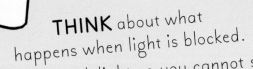

THINK about what happens when light is blocked.
- Bricks block light so you cannot see through walls.
- Glass does not block light. It is used to make windows and doors.

What other materials block out light?

YOU WILL NEED
Scissors
A shoebox
A ruler
A small toy
A small flashlight
Tape
A book
Some test materials (e.g. pieces of paper, cloth, clear plastic, plastic wrap, aluminum foil, tissue paper)
A pencil and paper

WHICH MATERIALS BLOCK OUT LIGHT?

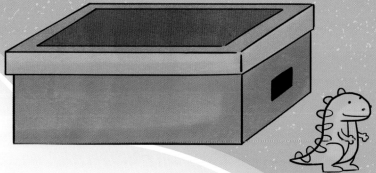

1 Ask an adult to cut a large hole in the top of the shoebox lid, and a small square hole in one side of the box, as shown here.

2 Put the toy inside the box and put the lid on.

3 Position the end of the flashlight over the hole in the side and tape it securely to hold it in place. You may need to rest the flashlight on something, such as a book. Switch it on.

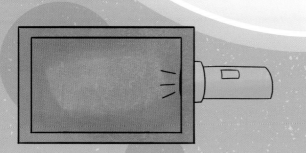

4 Lay your test materials, one at a time, over the hole in the lid, completely covering it. What can you see? Make a record of the results.

" BECAUSE...

You can see the flashlight and toy clearly through some materials. This is because almost all the light passes through these materials, from inside and outside the box. These materials are **transparent.**

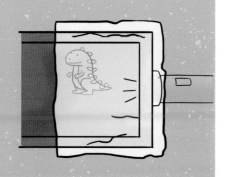

Some materials let some light through them but block the rest. You can see the flashlight glowing inside the box, but you cannot see the toy very clearly.
These materials are **translucent.**

The other materials block all of the light, both from outside and inside the box. You cannot see inside the box at all. These materials are **opaque.**

"

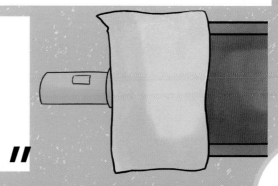

19

MAKING SHADOWS

When an object blocks out light it makes a **shadow**.

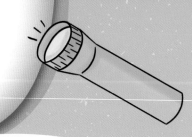

THINK about how objects make shadows.
- Look under your bed. Is it dark there? The darkness is a shadow made by the bed.
- Turn on a desk lamp. Do the objects under the light have shadows? How do objects make shadows?

YOU WILL NEED

The shoebox and book from pages 18–19
A paintbrush and some black paint
A large plastic comb
Tape
A flashlight

HOW ARE SHADOWS MADE?

1. Remove the lid, toy, and flashlight from the shoebox. Paint the inside of the box. with black paint.

" BECAUSE...

You see striped shadows in the box because the teeth of the comb block the flashlight. Light travels in straight lines. It cannot bend around the teeth of the comb to shine behind them.

Some shadows are stronger than others. A glass cup is transparent. It will make a shadow but the shadow is weak. Put something solid, such as a straw, inside the glass and you will see its shadow through the glass. A teacup or mug is opaque. It blocks light, so its shadow is strong. If something is inside the mug you cannot see its shadow through the mug. "

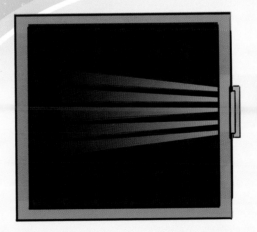

2 Tape the plastic comb over the hole in the side of the box.

3 Position your flashlight on the book and shine it through the comb and through the hole. What can you see?

SHADOW SHAPES

An object's shadow is a similar shape to the object.

THINK about how shadows look.

- The shadow a ball makes is round like the ball.
- The shadow your hand makes is shaped like your hand.

Can shadows change their shape?

YOU WILL NEED

A helpful adult

Scissors

The same shoebox as before

A plain white plastic bag

Tape

A book

A small flashlight

A chair

Some friends

A collection of small objects

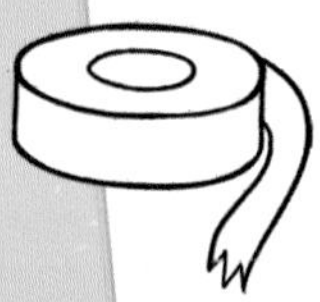

WHAT SHAPES DO SHADOWS MAKE?

1 Ask an adult to cut out the base of the shoebox, leaving a 0.5-inch (1.25 cm) rim.

2 Cut a piece of the plastic bag to cover the base of the box. Stretch the plastic over the base and tape it firmly around the sides. This is your screen.

3 Stand the box upright with the screen facing away from you. Put a book inside it to weigh it down.

4 Place the flashlight behind the screen so that it shines into the box. It may need to rest on something.

5 Ask your friends to sit in front of the screen. Darken the room. Put each object, one at a time, in front of the flashlight so that it makes a shadow on the screen.

6 Can your friends guess what each object is? Move the object closer to the flashlight and then further away. What happens to its shadow?

"BECAUSE...

Shadows can play tricks on your eyes because all you see is a flat outline of the object. If the object is turned at an angle to the light, the shadow you see may be squashed or stretched out. If an object is close to the light source, its shadow is larger. If it is further away, its shadow is smaller. "

SUN AND SHADOW

Shadows happen outdoors, too.

THINK about when you can see shadows outside.

- Are there shadows on a cloudy day?
- Are there shadows on a sunny day? What kinds of shadow does sunlight make?

YOU WILL NEED
A sunny day
A friend

BECAUSE...

The best shadows happen on clear, sunny days when the Sun's light shines directly on the ground. Any object that stands between the Sun and the ground forms a shadow on the opposite side to the Sun.

HOW DOES THE SUN MAKE SHADOWS?

1 Go outside with a friend on a sunny day. What shadows do you see?

2 Stand in an open space with your back to the Sun. Where is your shadow?

HOW DO THE SUN'S SHADOWS CHANGE?

1 Stand outside in a sunny spot early in the morning. Ask a friend to make a chalk mark on the ground where your shadow ends.

YOU WILL NEED
A friend
An open spot
Chalk

2 Come back to the same spot at midday and mark your shadow again. Has it changed?

" BECAUSE...

Your shadow is longer in the early morning because the Sun is low in the sky. At midday, the Sun is almost straight above you and your shadow is much shorter. It is also pointing in a different direction than your morning shadow. Why is that? "

25

SHIFTING SHADOWS

Shadows from sunlight point in different directions at different times of day.

THINK about how the Sun's shadows change.
- Which side of your house is in shadow in the morning?
- Which side is in shadow in the evening?

Have the shadows moved?

YOU WILL NEED
A sunny morning
A piece of cardboard
A straight stick
Sticky tack
An open piece of ground
A ruler and a marking pen
A clock

HOW DO THE SUN'S SHADOWS MOVE?

1 Start early in the morning.

2 Make a hole in the middle of the card. Push the stick through the card and into the ground so it is held in place.

3 Use the ruler and the marking pen to draw along the stick's shadow on the card. Write the time at the end of the shadow. Be careful not to move the card or the stick.

4 Come back every two hours. Mark where the shadow is each time and write the time down. How does the stick's shadow move during the day?

Long ago, people used the movement of the Sun's shadows to tell the time. Shadow clocks are called **sundials**.

9 A.M.

" BECAUSE...

Shadows always point away from the light source that is making them. The stick's shadow moved around the card because the direction of the Sun's light changed during the day. **"**

GLOSSARY

Artificial light sources

are light sources made by people. They do not exist naturally. For example, candles and electric lights would not exist if we did not make them.

The Moon

is a ball of rock that travels around Earth. We see it in the sky because the Sun's light bounces off it and shines down to Earth. Unlike the Sun, the Moon does not make any light of its own.

Natural light sources

are light sources that happen in nature, such as the Sun. A few animals, such as glowworms and fireflies, make their own light. Lightning is a short but very powerful burst of natural light.

Opaque

materials are things that we cannot see through at all. They reflect all of the light that falls on them. Stone and wood are opaque materials. Most of our clothes are opaque, too!

Pupils

are the dark holes in the middle of the colored parts of our eyes. Light shines through our pupils onto the back of our eyeballs. Our brain then tells us what we are seeing.

Reflected light

is the light that bounces off the surface of things. We see things because light is bouncing off them and into our eyes. Mirrors reflect light so well that we see a perfect, reversed copy of ourselves when we look into them.

Senses

allow us to find out what is happening around us. We have five senses. They are seeing, hearing, touching, tasting, and smelling.

Shadows

are the dark areas that form behind objects when they block out light.

The Sun

is a gigantic ball of glowing gas that gives out great amounts of light and heat. It is more than 100 times bigger than Earth and is about 93 million miles (150 million km) away. It takes eight minutes for light from the Sun to reach Earth.

Sundials

were used by people long ago to tell the time. Sundials work using shadows cast by the Sun's light. These shadows change during the day because the Earth is turning. It takes 24 hours for the Earth to make a complete turn.

Translucent

materials allow us to see light through them, but not much else. These materials let some light pass through them but they reflect the rest. Tracing paper and frosted glass are translucent.

Transparent

materials are things that we can see through clearly. Most of the light that falls on them passes through them. Glass and water are transparent.

LEARNING MORE

BOOKS

Claybourne, Anna. *Recreate Discoveries about Light.* Crabtree Publishing, 2019.

Johnson, Robin. *The Science of Light Waves.* Crabtree Publishing, 2017.

Solway, Andrew. *From Sunlight to Blockbuster Movies: An Energy Journey Through the World of Light.* Capstone Publishing, 2015.

WEBSITES

Find out some more cool facts about light, at:

www.pbs.org/video/light-is-waves-crash-course-physics-39-reswy6/

Explore light, videos, games, experiments, and much more about light at:

www.sciencekids.co.nz/light.html

PLACES TO VISIT

Visit the Shadow Wall and Everbright Interactive Light Wall at The Hands-ON! Regional Museum in Johnson City, Tennessee. Check out their discovery on the go STEM programs at www.visithandson.org

NOTE TO PARENTS AND TEACHERS:

Every effort has been made by the publisher to ensure that these websites contain no inappropriate or offensive material. However, because of the nature of the Internet, it is impossible to guarantee that the content of these sites will not be altered. We strongly recommend that Internet access is supervised by a responsible adult.

INDEX

beams of light 14, 15
bending light 15, 21
blocking light 7, 11, 18, 19, 29
brightness 9, 10, 13
burning 13

candles 13, 28
clouds 10, 11, 24

darkness 6, 9, 12, 16, 20, 23
daytime and daylight 6, 10, 11

Earth 29
electric lights 12, 13, 20, 28
eyes 6, 8, 9, 10, 16, 23, 28

fireflies 28
firelight 13, 28
flashlights 12, 14, 15, 16, 19, 20, 21, 22

glass 18, 21, 29
glowworms 28

light sources 12, 13, 14, 23, 27, 28
lightning 28

midday 25
mirrors 9, 17, 28
Moon 13, 28

night 6, 12

opaque materials 19, 21, 28

pupils 8, 9, 28

reflected light 13, 16, 17, 19, 28, 29

seeing 6, 7, 8, 18, 28
senses 7, 28
shadows 20, 21, 22, 23, 24, 25, 26, 27, 29

Sun 10, 11, 12, 13, 24, 25, 26, 27, 28, 29
sundials 27, 29
sunlight 10, 12, 14, 24, 26

translucent materials 19, 29
transparent materials 19, 21, 29
traveling light 14, 15, 21